Russel Howcroft is _ _ _ _ _ a
personalities, and a regular panellist on ABC TV's high
rating *Gruen*, hosted by Wil Anderson. He co-wrote and
presented a documentary on Australian advertising legends
(and creators of the iconic 'Come on Aussie, come on!' and
many more famous jingles) Mo and Jo. A former Partner
and Chief Creative Officer at PwC, Russel is now the co-host
of Melbourne's number one breakfast show on 3AW, the
chair of AFTRS (Australian Film Television and Radio School),
a former board member of the Melbourne Football Club
and newly appointed member of the Melbourne Cricket
Club committee. Russel's first two books, *When It's Right
to be Wrong* and *The Right-brain Workout*, were bestsellers
for Penguin.

Alex Wadelton is an advertising writer turned social
activist turned author turned podcast host. He's created
advertising campaigns that have run all over the world
for clients such as the AFL, Cricket Australia, Wrigley's,
The University of Melbourne, Gatorade, and Schweppes.
He's raised hundreds of thousands of dollars for a range
of charities, was the driving force behind the Nicky Winmar
statue, and is the co-creator of Future Landfill. His first
book with Russel, *The Right-brain Workout*, was a bestseller.
He hosts The Right-brain Warm-up podcast, where he
interviews creative people about their habits, skills and
right-brain tips. He's also a dead ringer for Balki Bartokomous
from *Perfect Strangers*.

all new
questions to
re-train your
brain to be
more creative
in 10 weeks

the right-brain work out

2

Russel Howcroft
with **Alex Wadelton**

PENGUIN BOOKS

PENGUIN BOOKS

UK | USA | Canada | Ireland | Australia
India | New Zealand | South Africa | China

Penguin Books is part of the Penguin Random House group of companies
whose addresses can be found at global.penguinrandomhouse.com.

Penguin
Random House
Australia

First published by Penguin Books, 2020

Cover and internal design by Adam Laszczuk © Penguin Random House Australia Pty Ltd

Cover image by erattan/shutterstock.com

Internal images: pages 11 (moon surface by tereez/shutterstock.com); 18 (pattern by solarus/shutterstock.
com); 20 (bowling ball by Inked Pixels/shutterstock.com); 27 (heart by Olga Bolbot/shutterstock.com);
39 (sneakers by mama-mia/shutterstock.com); 61 (cassette by Dmitry Naumov/shutterstock.com and
handwritten graffiti font by Doozie Dozer/shutterstock.com); 65 (fly by irin-k/shutterstock.com);
66 (tree by Anna Kutukova/shutterstock.com); 75 (cobwebs by Gluiki/shutterstock.com); 105 (newspaper
by Feng Yu/shutterstock.com); 106 (crocodile image by NinkaStudio/shutterstock.com).

Printed and bound in China by 1010 Printing International Co Ltd.

A catalogue record for this
book is available from the
National Library of Australia

NATIONAL
LIBRARY
OF AUSTRALIA

ISBN 978 1 76089 9479

A proportion of the authors' royalties will be donated to Epilepsy Action Australia.
epilepsy.org.au

Epilepsy
Action
Australia

penguin.com.au

**Don't let anyone tell you
you're not creative**

Creativity. Innovation. And changing the world.

Nell Greenwood, CEO of the Australian Film Television and Radio School (of which I am the chair), was recently talking to me about the nature of creativity and the difference between creativity and innovation, as well as the need for the school to better understand and teach what creativity actually is.

During our chat Nell gave me an insight into how she likes to think about creativity. Her explanation has stayed with me ever since.

She described the three types of creativity to me.

The first is **small c**. This is the creativity innate to all human beings. The creativity that George Land's research proved was present in every single child he tested (as discussed in the first volume of *The Right-brain Workout*).

Secondly, there is **Professional c**, the creativity that individuals are able to exercise in their professional endeavours. Whether it's garden design, film directing or poetry composition, Professional c is the deployment of a creative skill for financial gain.

Finally, there is the **Big C**. The out-of-the-box, once-in-a-generation, oddball and precocious creativity that can literally change how we see the world. We are talking Michelangelo, Björk, Jørn Utzon, Coco Chanel and Frank Gehry levels of creativity.

Nell's explanation resonated with me because I suspect many of us have our creativity whittled away through conventional education, while we benchmark ourselves against the scary and rare Big C. 'They're not very creative' is a phrase we often hear when parents consider their children's skills (or lack thereof).

The thing is, we are comparing ourselves and our peers to the stand-out creativity that grabs headlines and sticks in our minds, instead of the everyday minor moments of ingenuity. After all, it's difficult for a parent to say how wonderful their child's artwork is when they're using their favourite painting at the National Gallery as the baseline!

I grew up in an interesting household. My father was a highly creative man: a cartoonist, artist, self-taught dodgy pianist, joke writer, singer (reasonable), dancer (almost reasonable), and general innovator and creator. He was a part-time Professional c with dreams of the Big C.

Each week he would draw a cartoon with his character Sam the Ram for the rural industry newspaper, *Stock and Land*. And from a very young age he would present me with three ideas and ask me to choose the best one. I don't recall if he listened to my point of view, but it certainly trained me to have one on creative work and the power of a good idea.

However, all this creativity meant there was a downside for me and my siblings, because we all benchmarked ourselves against our father . . . and he was hard to beat! We all had creative capability but none of us really stretched ourselves in an attempt to find that full Big-C potential.

And this is the trick. This is the important message of the second volume of *The Right-brain Workout*. There is no right idea, no single answer; there is no formula, no method, no scripture, no structure or sequence that must be adhered to.

So dive in, practise your small c, aspire to the Professional c and who knows, a full ten weeks of right-brain workouts just might lead to the Big-C breakthrough that changes how you see the world.

Russel Howcroft

just
imag

ine....

A kitten wrestling with a chicken on top of a fifty-storey building at dusk, on Mars, while a crowd of fluffy toys looks on.

You can picture that in your mind right now, can't you?

The amazing thing is, what you are imagining will be different to everybody else who has read the exact same sentence. Because some detail is bound to be different.

What fluffy toys do you see? What is the building made of? What breed of kitten is it? Who's winning? The variations are infinite in the human mind.

It shows that human imagination is a powerful force.

And it's something that separates us from all other creatures with whom we share this planet.

By being able to imagine concepts in our minds, the human race has been able to create all manner of physical things that have altered the course of our existence.

We have flown to the moon, developed astonishingly complex feats of engineering, invented intricate cuisine, constructed vast urban settlements with millions of inhabitants, produced opera, cinema and sculpture with the power to move people emotionally, and written literature that inspires all over the world.

We can summon running water at the flick of a wrist, electricity at the flick of a button, and through small rectangular handheld devices can call up any fact from history at the touch of a finger (or a voice command!).

It's really quite staggering when you stop and think for a minute.

And all of it stems from creativity.

Scientists being **creative**.

Engineers being **creative**.

Designers being **creative**.

Writers being **creative**.

Town planners being **creative**.

Humans being **creative**.

This second volume of *The Right-brain Workout* is designed to help you be more creative, no matter who you are, your age and tastes, or where you think your strengths lie.

So, pick up a pen or a pencil, sharpen your mind, and get stuck in. You never know what you might create after you've worked out your right side!

Alex Wadelton

let's

go!

week.01

01. food that rocks

Think of an album. That album is now a restaurant. The artist is the chef and each song is a dish on the menu. Your job is to design the menu, with descriptions for what's served as entree, main and dessert.

name: _____ chef: _____

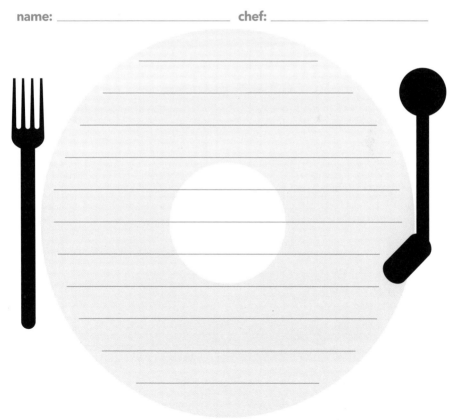

02. get drawn in

Produce a self-portrait using the opposite hand to the one you draw with. If you're ambidextrous, try using your toes.

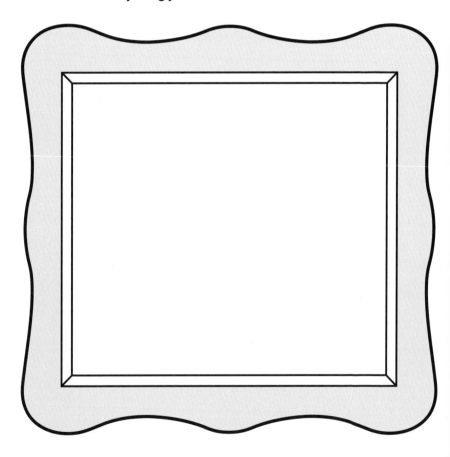

03.   unpossible

How do you get a messy child to clean
their room without being asked?

_____

_____

_____

_____

_____

_____

_____

_____

_____

_____

_____

_____

04. far out!

You are a far-right extremist with a shaved head.
What can you do to practise empathy?

_____

_____

_____

_____

_____

_____

_____

_____

_____

_____

_____

05. 24-carrot magic in the air

You bite into a carrot, only to find out that it talks. You form a close friendship that spans twenty years. This carrot knows you better than anyone else, and you, it. It's getting married. You're the best man/maid of honour. Write your speech.

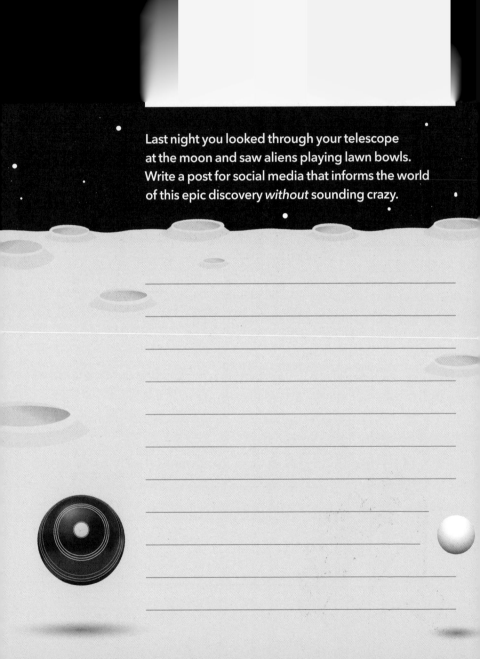

Last night you looked through your telescope
at the moon and saw aliens playing lawn bowls.
Write a post for social media that informs the world
of this epic discovery *without* sounding crazy.

07. boogie wonderland

Describe the new dance craze, 'dunzing'.

play with a balloon

week 01.
right-brain tip

There's something magical about reliving an experience that delighted you as a child. The gentle tap, tap, tap to keep a balloon in the air can put you right in the moment, resting your brain from analytical thought, and freeing the mind to make new connections.

week.02

08. spice it up

Greet your friends for a day with the following phrase.
'Hello, Barramundi. How are you going, Pretzel?'
What were your five favourite reactions?

1. _____

_____

2. _____

_____

3. _____

_____

4. _____

_____

5. _____

_____

09. on the spot

Open the 'Photos' app on your phone. Count back nine images. This photo has just been awarded the famed Golden Lion at the Venice Biennale. Congratulations. The first question you are asked at the press conference is,

'Why do you think this work has had such a strong reaction from the public for its representation of the current human condition?'

_____

_____

_____

_____

_____

_____

_____

_____

_____

_____

_____

10. drop the beat

If you had to replace your heartbeat with a drumming breakbeat, how would you use the high hat, snare, and bass drum?

11. POTUS (pen of the u.s.)

Imagine you were the White House biro used by the last four US presidents. Between their fingers of power, you danced across documents, making and breaking different laws. Now you're retired, a local journalist wants to write your biography. They want to know how you feel about everything you've ever done. They want to know what it's really like to be you. They ask: 'What biscuit best represents your personality, and why?'

MAKE COOKIES GREAT AGAIN

12. and on the 7th day

When God created the earth, was seven days
back then the same length as seven days today?
How would you convince an atheist of your answer?

_____

_____

_____

_____

_____

_____

_____

_____

_____

_____

_____

_____

_____

13.

back in five

Choose three words that rhyme with show.
Think of two words that rhyme with tell.
Now make a poem with your five new words.

show: 1. _____   tell: 1. _____

2. _____   2. _____

3. _____

_____

_____

_____

_____

_____

_____

_____

_____

_____

_____

_____

out of this world

If you were to open an organic space-food company that supplies people on Mars, what would you call it and what would be the tagline to promote it in advertisements?

set your phone to black and white

week 02.
right-brain tip

The bright colours of your phone encourage subconscious decisions and excite your brain to keep checking it. Remove the colour, and you'll find you use your phone less, and engage in the real world more. This will help you sleep better, and think more clearly.

week.03

15. child's play

Describe what you do for a living so it makes sense to a three-year-old.

what: _____

_____

_____

_____

_____

_____

_____

_____

_____

_____

16. i love me, i love me not

Pick your favourite part of your body.
Write it a love letter or poem.

Now pick the most troublesome part of your body.
Write it a break-up letter.

17. three fine mice

A group of mice have become intelligent and instead of taking over the world they start teaching a philosophy class. What subject do they cover in their first lesson?

_____

_____

_____

_____

_____

_____

_____

_____

_____

_____

18. shaken, not stirred

Turn your favourite song into a cocktail recipe.

19. foot-in-mouth disease

How would you go on with day-to-day life if your hands were your feet, and your feet were your hands?

_____

_____

_____

_____

_____

_____

_____

_____

_____

_____

20. everything is awesome

Name five ways LEGO could save the world.

1.

2.

3.

4.

5.

21.

no, no, no, yes

If there were a public holiday on 29 February,
what should we celebrate?

smile
first

week 03.
right-
brain
tip

We're conditioned to wait for someone else to smile first. So, try walking down the street and smiling at random people as you go. You might feel self-conscious at first, but soon you may feel a positive glow reflected back that opens up your mind to fresh thought.

week.04

22. dayte night

Pick a day of the week, and write a dating profile for it.

. . . . day

23. going loco

A man from the Stone Age travels into the future and appears in Japan. He sees a silver high-speed train zooming through a mountain at 320 km/h. In an instant, he's teleported back in time to where he came from. How does he describe what he saw to his friends?

24. sit-down comedy

Write one minute of the worst stand-up comedy you can on this page. Then convince a friend or family member that you want to try stand-up comedy and perform it for them. Secretly record their reaction, and you've got yourself a hilarious video!

25. in a flap

If you could give a kookaburra any other type of laugh, what would it be and why?

what: _____

why: _____

_____

_____

_____

_____

_____

_____

_____

_____

_____

26. so hot right now

You just woke up and checked your phone.
You have 1,000,987,980 friend requests.
So what did you get up to last night, eh?

1,000,987,980

27. silver linings

Describe a rainbow to someone who doesn't understand colour.

_____

_____

_____

_____

_____

_____

_____

_____

_____

_____

_____

28. super duper

Design your superhero outfit, and then come up with a catchphrase and special power.

float

week 04.
right-brain tip

Flotation therapy can reset your body and mind in under sixty minutes. The weightlessness and complete darkness are in stark contrast to the hectic outside world and are ideal conditions to let your mind wander. It's the closest thing you can find to floating in the stars. Get in touch with the universe. Go float.

week.05

29. **blankety blanks**

Fill in the blanks in this story. It need not make any sense. Try it again, creating a new nonsense tale. Finally, fill in the blanks as quickly as possible.

I set out from ...., and rode on a .... all the way to .... There I met a .... named ...., who offered me a cheap .... which I immediately .... It made me feel really .... Suddenly, I became desperate for a .... However, all I could find was a .... 'What a .... day,' I said.

I set out from ...., and rode on a .... all the way to .... There I met a .... named ...., who offered me a cheap .... which I immediately .... It made me feel really .... Suddenly, I became desperate for a .... However, all I could find was a .... 'What a .... day,' I said.

I set out from ...., and rode on a .... all the way to .... There I met a .... named ...., who offered me a cheap .... which I immediately .... It made me feel really .... Suddenly, I became desperate for a .... However, all I could find was a .... 'What a .... day,' I said.

30. magic carpet

You have to design a simple carpet that can move of its own volition. How do you do it?

31. a snowflake's chance

A snowflake will take about sixty years from when it lands at the top of the Franz Josef Glacier to be carried by the ice to the end of the glacier. Describe what it's thinking at the start of that journey.

32.

Name your favourite film: _____

_____

Write a summary of the plot in a paragraph: _____

_____

_____

_____

_____

_____

_____

_____

_____

Now write it in a sentence: _____

_____

_____

_____

Now write it in just six words: _____

_____

33. holey moley!

You awaken to find a large hole in your back garden so deep you can't see the bottom. A ladder leads into the darkness. What do you discover when you climb down?

_____

_____

_____

_____

_____

_____

_____

_____

_____

_____

_____

_____

34. wish you were here?

You've just arrived on Earth for the first time from another galaxy for a 'holiday'. What do you write about your first impressions of life on Earth and its Earthling inhabitants to your friends and family on your home planet?

spacemail

35. dig that music

Palaeontologists are always getting things wrong. We grew up thinking dinosaurs were super badass lizards and then they tried telling us they were actually giant chickens. It's now been discovered that dinosaurs did not engage in combat, but in fact settled their differences via rap battle. A T-rex has just accidentally trampled a stegosaurus's vegetable garden. You are the stegosaurus. Drop your verse.

take a different route to work

week 05.
right-
brain
tip

It's good to break out of your routine every now and then. Mix up your daily commute by getting off at a different stop and walking to the office through back streets, or drive on a different road. You never know what you might find around that next corner.

week**.06**

36. freaky flyday

You wake to discover you've been switched into the body of a fly. How do you alert your family without getting yourself killed?

s#*t

37. like birds of a feather

Draw a treehouse that the person you most admire would design for pigeons.

_____

_____

_____

_____

_____

_____

_____

_____

_____

_____

_____

Imagine gravity is in reverse, so instead of being attracted to the earth, you are repelled. How would you design a transport system to get around?

38. **what comes down, must go up**

39. 100 words to set you free

Learn to see what's important in the world; the magic that's hidden beneath the veneer of the everyday. Look at what's happening right now in front of you. Then, look deeper. What's under the surface? Next, write one hundred words about it in ten ten-word sentences.

10 + _____

10 + _____

10 + _____

10 + _____

10 + _____

10 + _____

10 + _____

10 + _____

10 + _____

10 + _____ = 100

40. the re-cycle

You have been given a brief by Elon Musk to launch his new really fast motorbike that runs entirely on rubbish. He wants to say: 'This is a really fast motorbike that runs entirely on rubbish.' Give him eight options that say it in new and original ways.

41.

shake it up, shake it up

Describe your favourite song as a milkshake.

42. it is written

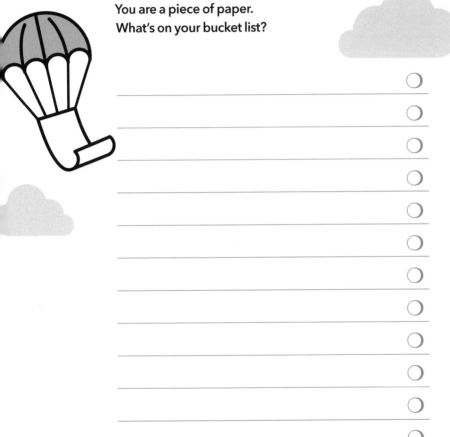

You are a piece of paper.
What's on your bucket list?

○
_____
○
_____
○
_____
○
_____
○
_____
○
_____
○
_____
○
_____
○
_____
○
_____
○
_____
○
_____
○
_____

look deep into an eye

week 06.
right-brain tip

It could be your own eye. Or a loved one's. When you stare into an eye, your mind slows down, and you are lost in the infinite depth of the soul. What is important in life? Why are we here? Open yourself to weighing up such questions and see how it makes you feel.

week.07

43. web of intrigue

You wake up in your house during a period of prolonged self-isolation to discover your children have turned into spiders. What happens next?

_____

_____

_____

_____

_____

_____

_____

_____

_____

_____

_____

_____

_____

44. same same but different

Think of a story you tell often, the kind of thing you might bring out at a dinner party. How would you tell it if you had to cut it down to thirty seconds? And how would you tell it if you had to stretch it to an hour?

30 sec: _____

1 hr: _____

45. instant endorsement

Congratulations! You've scored a meeting with the internet's best influencer. How do you convince them to endorse your latest invention, the quandoniumozilite?

WOW!

A quandoniumozilite!!! WFT?

😍

I WANT ! I WANT!!

rubbish

this is great. where can i get one

OMG

you are soooo influential. i'll have one

❤️

a quadazoddle what???

I'm on team Q!

pft! mine broke.

46. woc oom

Draw a cow inside out.
Now describe how you would milk it.

now how: _____

_____

_____

_____

_____

_____

47. worm has turned

How could the late worm catch the early bird?

48. futurespeak

Imagine that a time traveller from fifty years in the future calls you. Describe your world right now to them.

hi

49. dr. do a lot

If all animals could suddenly talk but only for one day, who would you chat to, and what would you ask them?

who: _____

what: _____

_____

_____

_____

_____

_____

_____

_____

_____

_____

right-brain news

smell
the
flowers

week 07.
right-brain tip

New smells stimulate the 'new experiences' part of the brain and can lift your mood. And when you're happier you can concentrate more on the task at hand, instead of focusing on things that are wrong.

week.08

50. two-hit wonder

Write the chorus for the sequel to your favourite song. For example, if your favourite song is Beyoncé's 'Single Ladies (Put a Ring on It)' you might say, 'He did eventually put a ring on it. Then the drinking started.'

fave song: _____

new song: _____

chorus: _____

_____

_____

_____

_____

_____

_____

_____

_____

_____

_____

upside down, miss jane

Draw a bowl of fruit from a photo that's upside down. When you're finished, turn it back around and see how you did. Now, draw it the right way up.

51.

52. note to 15-year-old self

Remember that Slurpee that transported you back in time so you could slip a note to your younger self? Well, turns out it was poison and you're now dying. What are your dying words that you want the world to remember you by?

53. a beautiful choir

Imagine a group of people singing. What is the strangest thing that could happen as they sing? For example, perhaps a bird starts singing with them and a whole flock joins in to create an amazing harmony!

54. it's alive!

An inanimate object becomes alive.
What is it, and what is the impact of its existence?

_____

_____

_____

_____

_____

_____

_____

_____

_____

_____

_____

_____

_____

_____

_____

_____

55. build it up

You just inherited a block of land to build a house. But there is a catch. The land is the size of a single parking space. Thankfully the laws of physics don't apply and your budget is endless. Draw your creation.

56. beyond the wheel

Imagine yourself as a hamster. What kind of adventure could you have within your own house?

_____

_____

_____

_____

_____

_____

adventure land

_____

_____

_____

write a letter by hand

week 08.
right-
brain
tip

There is a lot of research showing that human connection is more important than ever, especially with technology seemingly all-pervasive. So, when you take the time to handwrite someone a letter, you are not only showing them you care, you'll also affect them more deeply than a text or email ever can.

week.09

57. and the winner is . . .

The inaugural 'World Changers' award – for people who've made undeniably game-changing innovations or discoveries – is to be given to Alexander Fleming, the physician who discovered penicillin. You think it should go to Peter Brinkworth, the bloke who invented chicken salt. Write a short speech on why Peter is the more worthy recipient.

58. gold, gold, gold

Describe the new, revolutionary swim stroke that you use to claim gold at the Olympics.

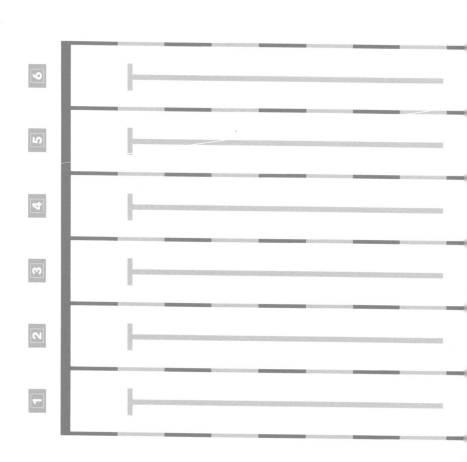

59. frowning bananas

You've just released a country music album with seven of the saddest songs you've ever written, all of which are about a banana. What is each track called?

1. _____

2. _____

3. _____

4. _____

5. _____

6. _____

7. _____

60. stand up, be heard

Write and design your protest banner
for a future rally you are passionate about.

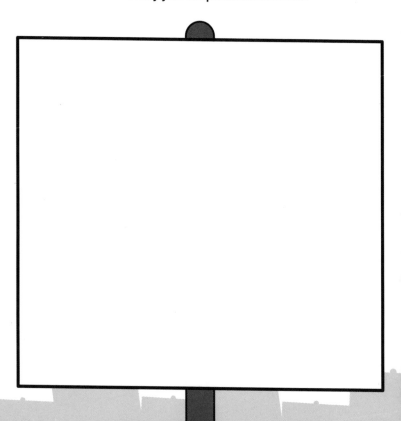

61. hatching ideas

What are a snow chicken's thoughts
while keeping its eggs warm?

62. north pole's most wanted

If Santa didn't have magical powers, describe how he would get into your house to deliver presents without being caught.

63. paws for thought

Draw your pet as a human.
If you don't have a pet, draw yourself as a pet.

do a
puzzle

week 09.
right-
brain
tip

Break yourself out of familiar thought patterns. Challenge your mind in a way that is completely different from what you do for your job. By concentrating so completely on finding a solution, you'll also be practising a form of mindfulness.

week.10

64. blow your top

Imagine Mount Everest were a volcano.
What would be the newspaper headline
if it were to erupt?

65. cute but deadly

Scientists have bred a cross between a crocodile and a koala. Name this new species. Write the voice-over for a short documentary on the animal's feeding habits.

66. some assembly required

IKEA has just launched the Mirräkel.
Create the instruction manual.

MIRRÄKEL

1.

2.

3.

4.

67. unearthed

Over millions of years, life on Earth has evolved from before the era of dinosaurs to the Stone Age and beyond to the modern world today. What's the name of a new bygone era you have just discovered, and five notable events in its history?

BIG BANG · DINOSAURS · STONE AGE · RUSSEL & ALEX · _____

1. _____

2. _____

3. _____

4. _____

5. _____

68. zombie feast

There is an outbreak of zombies. But they aren't interested in human brains ... What do they crave though, and why do they want it?

69. clink!

Using a chopstick and a glass, tap a rhythm that expresses the following emotions.

joy | **anxiety** | **embarrassment** | **curiosity**
exhaustion | **exhilaration**

What crossed your mind as you thought of the rhythm for each?

joy: _____

_____

anxiety: _____

_____

embarrassment: _____

_____

curiosity: _____

_____

exhaustion: _____

_____

exhilaration: _____

WOW!
WOW!
WOW!

the
right-
brain
work
out

best served . . .

If you were a beer or a wine, how would the label read on the back of the can/bottle?

_____

_____

_____

_____

_____

_____

_____

_____

_____

_____

_____

_____

_____

take care of a plant

week 10.
right-
brain
tip

Plants supply the oxygen we need to survive. So why not take a few minutes to care for something that cares for us? A quiet two minutes every day will help you know you've achieved something momentous. Maybe seeing your plant grow will be a quiet satisfaction.

well

done

Now . . . how are you going to use your creativity to change the world?

That's a big claim, to be sure.

But what is life for, other than to aim high?

When you aim high you can improve the lives of the people you love, achieve your goals, and give yourself lots of ways to enjoy your time here on earth.

Because being creative is just plain **FUN**. You can literally create something out of nothing with just the power of your mind. And the more you do it, the more fun you'll have and the stronger your creative side will be.

When you think about it, the best thing is that you'll **NEVER** be wrong. You'll simply have done something different.

That's what being a human is all about. Trying new things and never settling for the same old same old. After all, how else can you change the world?

bonus question.

You're invited to submit a question for the next edition of *The Right-brain Workout*. What is your question going to be?

?.

Send it to hello@rightbrainworkout.com.au and it might be included in the next book!

the right-brain brains trust

This book couldn't have happened without the wonderful contributions from the following creative legends. Many thanks to all of them who donated their time to pose the curly questions in *The Right-brain Workout 2*.

Question 1 – Adam Lock
Adam Lock is a creative director in the field of advertising. Adam's career has seen him work across three continents and on some of the most creative brands in the world including, Budweiser, Vodafone and Burger King.
adamglock.com

Question 2 – Andrew Fyfe
Andrew is a cartoonist, animator and creative best known for his live cartoons using the 'pen cam' on the television show *Hey Hey It's Saturday*. He went on to produce weekly animations for *The AFL Footy Show* and to co-host his own television gameshow *Guess What?* His work has appeared in advertising campaigns, theatrical productions and in publications including Australian *Mad Magazine*, the *Sunday Telegraph* and *TV Week*.
andrewfyfe.com.au

Question 3 – Angus Smallwood
Angus is a little bit right-brain and a little bit left. Google him. He's got a BSc, he's hosted a gameshow, he's written for cafe guides and he voiced the English translation of four characters in a Korean kids' animation. He now works as a brand strategist and a copywriter, helping define clients' problems and then solving them creatively.
thereactor.com.au

Question 4 - Stu Morley

Stu is a photographer and videographer working in and around beauty, fashion and advertising. He is also the director of Disco Studios in St Kilda, Melbourne, and runs the content production company Tiny Disco with his lovely wife Chelsea Morley.

stumorley.com

Question 5 - Chris Baker

Bakes is a creative director, strategist and, no matter what people say, he can in fact dunk a basketball too. I've seen him do it. It was awesome.

itsbakes.com

Question 6 - Professor Alan Duffy

Alan is an astronomer who creates baby universes on supercomputers to understand how galaxies like our Milky Way form within massive clouds of invisible dark matter. When not searching simulated universes, he tries to explain the science of this one onstage and on radio and TV.

alanrduffy.com

Question 7 - Jonny Clow

Jonny has over twenty years of experience in integrated advertising in London, Chicago and, now, Melbourne. He founded BD Network Australia in 2010 and has gone on to win numerous awards including the only Australian company to be recognised in Fast Company's 50 Best Workplaces for Innovators 2019, while the managing director of VERSA.

Question 8 - Heather Dinas

Heather is a professional photographer who specialises in lifestyle, food and the visual arts. Her work has been widely exhibited and she has featured as a finalist in the Head On Portrait Prize at the Australian Centre for Photography, the Josephine Ulrick and Win Schubert Photography Awards and in the Australian Photography Awards.

heatherdinas.com

Question 9 - Adam Luttick

Luts is a Melbourne-based photographer. His latest work, 'Everything Must Go', is a collection capturing stolen moments in time, where the confluence of people and objects weave themes of consumerism, inequality and alienation with tenderness. Luts chooses the most humble and whimsical of subjects to talk about chaos and design.
lutsphotography.com

Question 10 - Yianni Agisilaou

Yianni is a comedian who tours all around the world with a mind as sharp as a Ginsu blade. His ability to deliver smart but accessible laugh-packed material and also to improvise skilfully with whatever a room throws at him combine to create a truly unique experience.
ycomedian.com

Question 11 - Thomas Charles Hyland

Thomas is a director and writer who makes commercial, narrative and non-fiction work. He's made ads for the government, artwork for MONA, docos for SBS and potato dinners for his partner.
thomascharleshyland.com.au

Question 12 - Paul Baxter

Paul has more than 26 years' experience in audio post-production, and specialises in sound design and creating highly realistic soundscapes. He gathers many of his samples from the real world, instead of only relying on overused sound effects libraries.
baxtersound.com.au

Question 13 - Carolyn Tetaz

Carolyn is a prize-winning published poet, and was poetry editor for the international literary journal *Nocturnal Submissions*. She has been a book reviewer for *The Age* and *The Big Issue* and a feature writer for *Marie Claire*. While living in LA, Carolyn worked as a writer's assistant to writer and director Audrey Wells on several film and TV projects, and was writer-in-residence for Hello Sunshine, Reese Witherspoon's media company.

Question 14 – Andrea Clarke

Andrea is a recovering television news reporter who now works with companies wanting to build future-fit workforces. Her first book *Future Fit,* won the Australian Business Book of the Year.

careerceo.com.au

futurefitco.com.au

Question 15 – Nick Brown

Nick is the co-founder and executive creative director of Melbourne-based creative agency The Reactor. It's always been about advertising for Nick, citing the Italian Feast TV commercial for Little Caesars Pizza that started it all at the age of fourteen.

thereactor.com.au

Question 16 – Rambo Goraya

Rambo is a client-side creative director. He should probably get around to making a website to showcase his work.

Question 17 – Blair Panozza

Blair likes to think that the creative department of an advertising agency is his real home. A place where you look forward to returning to day in, day out, where no-one minds if you stroll around without pants. When he isn't creating ideas for you, he particularly enjoys writing poetry, cooking, and talking about himself in third person.

bpanozza.com

Question 18 – David Smith

David Smith is the founder of Blood UTD, where he works in the world's most powerful medium: sport.

bloodutd.com

Question 19 – Joe Round-Rawlins

Joey is a designer specialising in logo design, branding and user interface and user experience.

behance.net/josephround-r

Question 20 - Danish Chan

Danish is one of the most awarded creative strategists in the world, having worked on some of the most effective brands of the last decade. Today, Danish is a co-founder of untangld, a pragmatic brand and communication consultancy without the usual BS.
untangld.co

Question 21 - Mads Catanese

Mads is an account-service-person-turned-creative who believes creativity has the power to change the world.
madscatanese.com

Question 22 - Dave Thornton

Dave has built a global reputation for his honest, engaging, whip-smart and damn funny comedy. He's stormed the world's three major comedy festivals and, back home, Dave is a hot ticket across the country, filling thousands of seats with a growing army of fans.
❶ davethorntoncomedy

Question 23 - Marcus Byrne

Marcus is a multidisciplinary integrated designer and art director with a flair for high-end digital imaging and post-production retouching. Most weekends he can be found in Melbourne's music venues shooting live bands, wearing serious ear plugs and dodging crowd surfers.
behance.net/marcusbyrne

Question 24 - Tom Whitty

Tom is the creator and host of the *Time To Die* podcast, the unfunniest podcast you'll ever listen to, where comedians are challenged to write the worst routine of their life, and then get another comedian to perform it. He is also an award-winning journalist, composer and artist.
❶ TimeToDiePod

Question 25 - Steve Philp

Steve is a Sydney-based stand-up comedian originally from Newcastle who tells jokes on stages all over Australia and before TV shows start filming, such as *Ready Steady Cook*, *The NRL Footy Show*, and *Australia's Got Talent*.

 ComedianStevePhilp

Question 26 - Katie Britton

Katie is an award-winning advertising writer and the creative lead at food and beverage company Soulfresh with a disproportionately big right brain. Evidence of this can be found at **ideasbykatie.com**

Question 27 - Tara Ford

Tara is the multi-award-winning chief creative officer of advertising agency DDB Sydney. In between working with the teams to create iconic work for their clients, she squeezes in raising four spirited boys.

taraford.com

Question 28 - Lainie Chait

Lainie is an author, performer and stand-up comedian as well as a teacher in Animal Studies at TAFE. Her autobiography *Electro Girl* is about her almost two decade-long journey living a symbiotic existence with epilepsy.

electrogirl.com.au

Question 29 - Andrew Hansen

Andrew is an Australian comedian whose TV shows include *The Chaser's Election Desk*, *The Chaser's Media Circus*, *The Hamster Wheel*, *The Chaser's War On Everything*, and *CNNNN*. He's toured a bunch of live musical comedy shows around Australia, and made the ARIA-winning album *The Blow Parade*.

chaser.com.au

Question 30 - Emma Maxwell

Emma is considered one of Asia Pacific's foremost interior designers. Since founding Emma Maxwell Design in 2014, she has developed and refined her concept of modernism as a basis for design, which has seen her work recognised by many international awards.
emmamaxwelldesign.com

Question 31 - Denise Eriksen

Denise is co-founder, with Esther Coleman-Hawkins, of Media Mentors Australia. They help creatives create - through mentoring, workshops, conferences, networking events - by using their expertise from absurdly long careers telling stories in the creative world.
mediamentors.com.au

Question 32 - Damien Hashemi

Damien is a statistician, who became a graphic designer, who became an art director, who then became a behavioural researcher . . . and so is a statistician again. He's an odd Venn diagram of people who think they're good at Photoshop and spreadsheets.
damienhashemi.com

Question 33 - Michael Skarbek

Michael is a creative consultant. Having been in advertising agencies for fifteen years as a copywriter and creative director, he now works remotely, often while travelling the world and homeschooling his two children with his wife.
michaelskarbek.com

Question 34 - Julie Matthews

Julie is a creative director at OMD with more than twenty years' experience across five countries, including the UK, Singapore and China, working on some of the world's most loved brands such as Qantas, Telstra, L'Oréal, and McDonald's. When she isn't solving problems for global brands, Julie is giving university lectures in art direction, or spending time painting and drawing.
juliematthewscreative.com

Question 35 - Jess Wheeler

Jess is an internationally awarded writer, creative director and current state head of AWARD School. He holds no 'qualifications' for any of these titles and got into advertising after writing a Gumtree ad for an enchanted barbecue that went viral. His other accolades include being interviewed by *Rolling Stone* for building a Lena Dunham Apology Generator.

jessmakesads.com

Question 36 - John Pace

John subsidised his early directing career as a freelance creative in agencies in Australia and New York, writing commercials for Amazon, among others. That experience coupled with a buttload of time writing TV and film scripts has seen him take a unique approach to making ads, one which dovetails creative development and production.

hooves.com.au

Question 37 - Claire Salvetti

Claire Salvetti is an award-winning creative-industry-CEO-turned-coach who specialises in leadership for people who are counted on for their creativity. She believes that questions have the power to help people find unique solutions for the trickiest of challenges.

peepultreecoaching.com

Question 38 - Scott Leggo

Scott is a leading Australian landscape photographer and internationally award-winning artist. From the snow-covered heights of the Australian Alps to the deserts of the outback, his photos capture Australia at its iconic best.

scottleggo.com

Question 39 - Iain McLean

Iain McLean is an award-winning writer. He started out in the UK as a screenwriter working on independent productions. During a stint in Los Angeles he wrote for CBS and NBC as well as small production companies. For the past decade he has been working as a copywriter.

iainhmclean.com

Question 40 - Micah Walker

Micah is the co-founder and executive creative director of Bear Meets Eagle On Fire, a creative studio that helps good brands and people think and make things differently. Formerly a creative partner at Fallon London and creative director at Wieden+Kennedy Portland, his work has been recognised with over 180 international awards in design, art direction and advertising.

beareaglefire.com

Question 41 - Andrew Lloyd

Andrew is an ex-pharmacist-turned-entrepreneur who has created and developed many distribution businesses in the FMCG world, while attempting to herd four daughters at home.

Question 42 - Kevin Wilson

Kevin is a Wongai man from the Goldfields region of Western Australia. He is co-founder of Nani Creative, a graphic design partnership specialising in design for projects promoting Aboriginal tourism. Kevin also facilitates youth urban art workshops, establishing a link between young talent and exposure to the possibilities of creative career options.

⟨⟩ kevwilliem

scamperdesign.com/nani

Question 43 - Sheridan Wadelton

Sheridan has worked in the film and advertising production industry for more than twenty-five years. She has worked on a feature film that was shown in the Un certain regard section at the Cannes Film Festival, produced ARIA-winning film clips, made hundreds of TV commercials, and is mother to two lovely spider children.

Question 44 - Jack Druce

Jack is one of Australia's sharpest and most original comedians. His unique humour has led him to headline shows nationwide, perform at Splendour in the Grass and comedy festivals all over Australia, as well as writing for Channel 10's *The Project*.

jackdruce.com

Question 45 – Alita Harvey-Rodriguez

Alita is known as one of Australia's leading customer experience futurists and the brains behind multi-award-winning application-based training and consultancy provider, MI Academy.
milkit.com.au

Question 46 – Esther Clerehan

Esther is Australia's leading creative talent specialist. Which sounds more interesting than a recruiter.
clerehan.com

Question 47 – Nick Pearce

Nick is the CEO and co-founder of HoMie, a streetwear clothing social enterprise that supports young people affected by homelessness or hardship by equipping them with the skills, confidence and experiences to be more work-ready and better prepared for their future.
homie.com.au

Question 48 – David Wadelton

David is an artist who has worked across many media, including painting and photography. He is considered one of Australia's foremost modernist painters, and now as a photographer is documenting the forgotten Australia, milk bar by milk bar, and kitsch living room by kitsch living room. His first book *Suburban Baroque* is out now.
wadelton.online

Question 49 – Hugh Peachey

Hugh is a highly awarded photographer and director/DOP with more than fifteen years' experience in advertising and commercial photography. His photographic style ranges from quirky, hyper-real shots to whimsical and often dreamlike subjects.
hughpeachey.com

Question 50 - Luke Wallis

Luke is a head of content, writer and music tragic. He has written for the TV show *Rockwiz*, is a published author and has interviewed some of the biggest stars in the world including Mick Jagger, Rihanna and Matt Damon. Most intimidating moment: trying to put a lapel mic on Keith Richards.

lukewallis.com

Question 51 - Tony Banks

Tony is one of the most respected advertising art directors in Australian history. In a thirty-year career he has crafted some of the most memorable campaigns the nation has seen.

tonybanks.com.au

Question 52 - Nigel Camilleri

Nigel has had the privilege to travel the world and work with some fascinating people, from Andre Agassi to Gabriel Macht, and a variety of athletes, artists and high school students each with a unique story to tell, whether that comes to life in a documentary, TV series, photograph or vertical banner ad with no sound.

safari.global

Question 53 - Tania de Jong AM

Tania is a trailblazing Australian soprano, award-winning social entrepreneur, creative innovation catalyst and spiritual journey woman. She is one of Australia's most successful female entrepreneurs and innovators, and among the AFR's 100 Women of Influence and the 100 Australian Most Influential Entrepreneurs. Tania has released eleven albums and her TED Talk has sparked international interest.

taniadejong.com
creativeuniverse.com.au

Question 54 - Michelle DeKlerk

Michelle is a person-shaped and relatively normal illustrator and graphic designer.

🔘 **shell.dk**

Question 55 - Tony Prysten

Tony solves problems and makes the complex simple with design and creativity. He is currently head of product design and experience/ creative director at Yellowfin. He was previously head of digital and experience at McCann Australia and before that, co-founder and executive creative director of digital agency Igloo.

prysten.com

Question 56 - Tobias McCullagh

Others have described Tobias as an enigma within the advertising industry. He's still rather fresh within the industry, but always exercising his little grey cells for new ideas.

iamtobes.com

Question 57 - Tommy Little

Tommy is a comedian and dispenser of the finest dickheadery.

tommylittle.com.au

Question 58 - Claudia Howcroft

Claudia is an experienced branding and identity designer who is currently generating creative communications for award-winning sparkling water brand Capi.

howcroftdesigns.myportfolio.com

Question 59 - Harrison Toomey

Harrison is an advertising graduate, aspiring creative, and suit stylist. With a love for fashion and exercising his right brain, he hopes that he can prove to the world that creativity can be sexy.

harrisontoomey.com

Question 60 - Fabian Marrone

Fabian is the chief marketing officer at Monash University, and a key driver behind their 'If you don't like it, change it' platform. In 2019 he was named the Chief Marketing Officer of the Year by the Australian Marketing Institute.

monash.edu

Question 61 - Divya Abe

Divya Abe is a designer in the fields of digital, print, experiential, UI/UX, motion and art direction, and loves to bounce ideas around with teams. She believes that there is no prejudice to who can create.

Ⓞ divya.zip

Question 62 - Lila Rose Wadelton

Lila is a seven-year-old who loves rainbows, unicorns and her family.

Question 63 - Charlie Howcroft

Charlie is an advertising creative, graphic designer, animator and musician with Melbourne band The Brungas. His animation series, Isolation Animation, was developed during the COVID-19 pandemic.

Ⓕ brungasband

Ⓞ isolationanimation

Question 64 - Roarke Wadelton

Roarke is a ten-year-old kid who loves sport and especially cricket. He also loves music.

Question 65 - Andrea McCannon

Andrea is an actor, presenter, voice artist and filmmaker. She's also a committed foodie and travel junkie, and a lover of language and fluffy cats.

imdb.me/andreamccannon

Ⓞ andreamccannon_actor

Question 66 - Reece Ryan

Reece is a multidisciplinary creative director who has led major branding, campaign and digital transformation projects both locally and in the UK. A Swiss army knife of creative crafts, Reece leads the digital and design-led thinking across all major client work at Hardhat.

hardhat.com.au

Question 67 - Jamen Percy

Jamen is a part-time advertising creative and full-time dreamer. He has won many international awards and is an official photographer for the Burning Man organisation.

jamenpercy.com

Question 68 – Anna Fransson

Anna is a holistic- and strategic-thinking designer with a big interest in workplace culture and the people who shape it. Part of Anna's work as creative lead at Aginic focuses on connecting culture and brand in an engaging way, as they evolve over time.

annafransson.com

aginic.com

Question 69 – Chris Corby

Chris is a music producer, audio director, audio engineer and sound designer working in a broad range of professional environments over the last thirty years. His studio credits include record production with artists such as You Am I, The Mavis's and Trè Samuels, as well as TV audio direction and sound mixing for Australian shows *The Project*, *Have You Been Paying Attention?* and *The Logies*.

ccsounddesign.com.au

Question 70 – Shane Dawson

Shane's keen eye and love for ideation has kept him busy as a creative in both the advertising and brand-building space for more than sixteen years, since right around the time he realised playing professional basketball was never really an option. In that time, Shane's managed to win several creative awards but insists no matter how many versions of Photoshop there are, he won't lose the desire to still get on the tools.

dawsome.me

Bonus question – Dan Monheit

Dan is a co-founder of Hardhat, a creative agency built for today. Dan is also creator/host of the innovative Real Big Things event series, a seasoned presenter at global conferences including SXSW, a university guest lecturer and co-host of *Bad Decisions*, a behavioural economics podcast.

hardhat.com.au

baddecisions-podcast.com

acknowledgements

Russel Howcroft

Alex Wadelton is where all my thanks need to be directed.
The Right-brain Workout is his inspiration and his perspiration.
He wants to make a dent in the creative universe, and I am only
too happy to partner him in this endeavour.

Good on you, Alex.

Alex Wadelton

Everything has always existed forever. Just in another form.
When you look at this page, you are looking at matter that is
billions of years old. It has just taken on different forms. It has moved
through the universe, evolved, devolved, hibernated, grown, frozen,
shrunk, liquified, evaporated, rained down, solidified, swept across
trillions of galaxies, and somehow through some quirk of fate
become part of this small blue planet, its molecules rearranged an
almost infinite amount of times until it sits here before you as this
collection of paper and ink, that one day will be disposed of, and
metamorphose into the next stage of its endless journey. Or maybe
it won't. Maybe it hasn't. Maybe it's true. Maybe it's not. Just know
that it could and couldn't be at the same time, now and forever.

So, thank you to each and every one of you for taking time to be
here, right now, to read this page and for believing in the power
of creativity.

Additionally, a huge thanks to: Tom Whitty (for amassing a range
of questions for this volume, and for being a genius); my brother
Jon (for showing that going for your dreams is the only way to go);
The Muckers (for the good times); The Gutterz (for the laughs
and the meaning); Russel (for pushing creativity ever forward
and for making this whole shebangabang a reality); and most
importantly to my wife Sheridan, my son Roarke, and my daughter
Lila (for inspiring me to be a better person).